Contents

Getting Started

Page 24

Designs

14

Basic Link Love

Cuff: Page 46
Necklace: Page 18

20

Fishtail

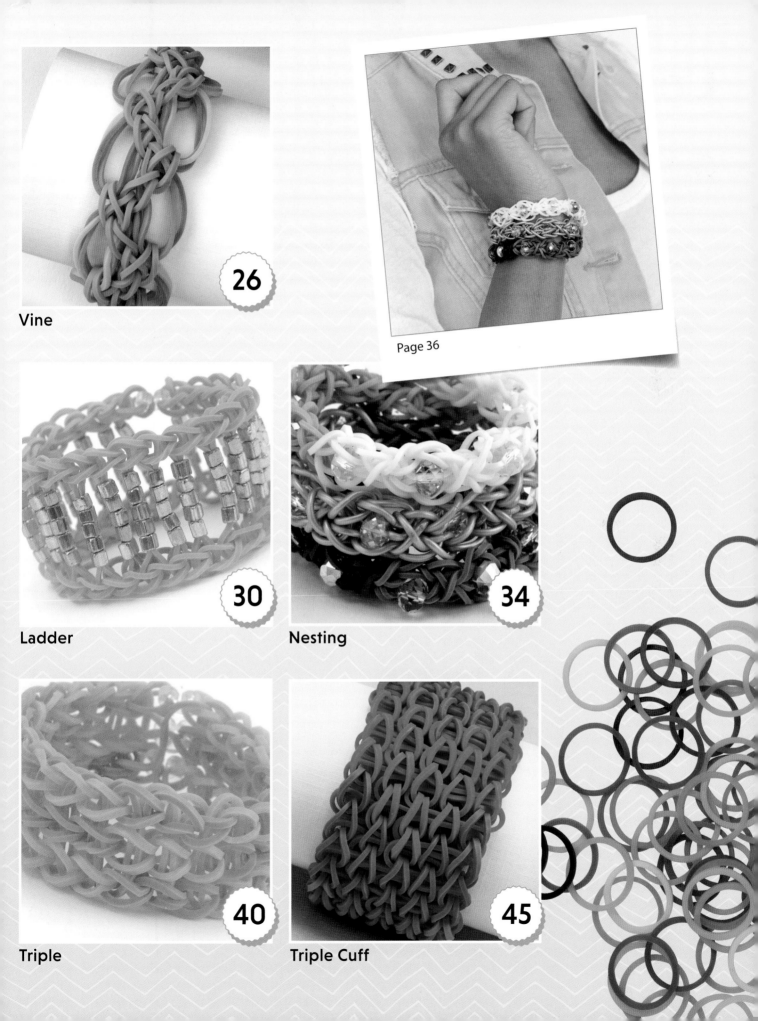

Vine

26

Page 36

Ladder

30

Nesting

34

Triple

40

Triple Cuff

45

Tools and Techniques

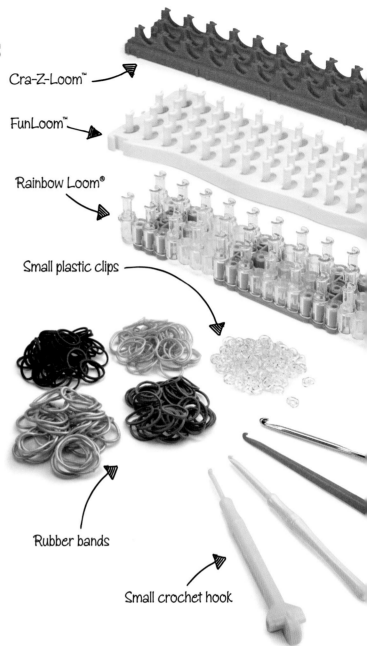

Cra-Z-Loom™

FunLoom™

Rainbow Loom®

Small plastic clips

Rubber bands

Small crochet hook

TOOLS AND MATERIALS

To get started, you'll need four basic items, most of which are available at your local craft store. You'll need:

☆ A loom for rubber band jewelry (such as Rainbow Loom®, Cra-Z-Loom™, or FunLoom™)

☆ Small plastic clips (C or S clips are best)

☆ Rubber bands (½" to ¾" [1.5 to 2cm] in diameter)

☆ A small crochet hook

To make the more ambitious and stylish projects in this book, you'll also need:

☆ A variety of beads

☆ Jewelry findings and closures

☆ Jewelry pliers, wire cutters, and scissors

☆ Thread

Looms can be purchased as kits that include all four of the basic items needed. Rubber bands, looms, clips, beads, and other tools and supplies can all be found online and at your local craft stores. Different looms have different numbers of rows or columns. All the projects and diagrams in this book show the Rainbow Loom®, but most projects are compatible with many looms. Simply follow the diagrams and instructions exactly; you may just have unused rows or columns of pegs.

USING JEWELRY FINDINGS AND CLIPS

To make your finished pieces look polished, use real jewelry findings like clasps, connectors, jump rings, split rings, and the like to complete your projects. That being said, the plastic clips that come with looms and bands are invaluable for use while your projects are still in progress, because they attach easily and don't fall off. Just keep the weight of the jewelry clasps in mind when choosing them; heavy ones might outweigh the bands, making for an unbalanced project, so sometimes just a simple jump ring is best.

MAKING BEADED BANDS WITH THREAD

A simple piece of sewing thread is your best friend when using beads for your pieces. Many beads have tiny holes that are impossible to thread thick rubber bands through with your fingers. But thread makes some of the tiniest holes workable. Cut a piece of thread about 9" (23cm) long; any longer and you'll waste time pulling the beads and bands onto it; any shorter and it will be difficult to keep a grip on and manipulate. Follow the instructions below to learn how to thread a bead onto a band.

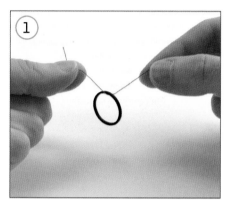

Thread one end of your thread through the rubber band that you want to bead.

Match the two thread ends together, and then twist or wet the ends so they stick together.

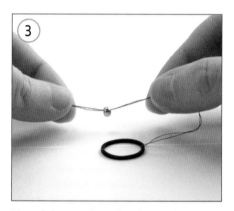

Thread the two thread ends together through a bead or beads, however many you want on the band.

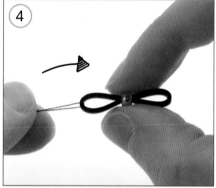

Holding the thread tightly in one hand, pull the bead(s) onto the band, stopping when the loops on either side of the bead are the same size. Don't be afraid to pull hard through stubborn beads.

BENDING AND CUTTING WIRE

Thin or thick jewelry wire can be used to create rubber band pieces that hold their shape. Use a strong jewelry wire cutter to snip wire lengths with one clean cut; if you have to squeeze repeatedly or bend the wire to get it to cut, you'll probably end up scratching the wire or creating a jagged end. Be careful when working with wire, as it's not pleasant to poke yourself under a fingernail (or anywhere) with a pointy end. You can use a metal file to smooth jagged or pointy wire ends or use needle nose pliers to curl the end back into the piece of jewelry so it doesn't scratch or snag clothing. When manipulating wire, nylon coated jewelry pliers will give you a cleaner look, as they don't scratch or indent the wire like metal pliers sometimes do.

WORKING WITH JUMP RINGS

Jump rings have a lot of uses in rubber band jewelry. They make great decorations when threaded on like beads; they can be used as links themselves, mixed in with rubber bands; they can be used to attach charms to a piece; and they are useful when attaching real jewelry closures. If you use jump rings as connectors or as permanently closed clasps, keep in mind the strength of the jump rings and how much you'll need to stretch a piece of jewelry. Repeatedly stretching a bracelet to put it on might eventually stretch open a weak jump ring, so consider using real jewelry clasps. Another option is to use split rings, which are much sturdier than jump rings. To use a split ring, simply use your pliers to pull apart the two coils of the split ring, and slide your bands onto the ring. (If you really love split rings and use them a lot, there are specialty split ring pliers that make separating the coils of the rings very easy.) The best way to work with jump rings is by using two pairs of jewelry pliers. Follow the tips below when manipulating jump rings.

Don't open the ring by pulling the two halves away from each other left and right. Doing it that way makes the ring lose its shape and can weaken the metal.

Use two pairs of pliers to open a jump ring. Position the jump ring with the split at the top, and use each pair of pliers to grip the ring on either side of the split.

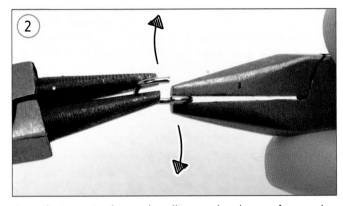

Open the jump ring by gently pulling one hand **toward** you and pushing the other **away**. To close a jump ring, slowly push it back the same way you opened it. **Do not** try to squeeze it closed using one pair of pliers.

MAKING SLIP KNOTS

Making slip knots is a useful technique for easily and permanently securing many bands together.

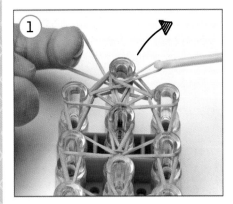

Using your hook, pull one end of a band through all the bands that you want to connect, holding the other end with a finger. In this example, you are completing a bracelet that has many bands on the top peg of the loom that need to be secured together.

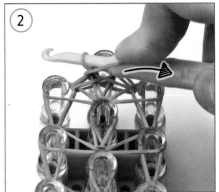

Loop the band on your finger onto the hook, placing it **behind** the band that's already on the hook.

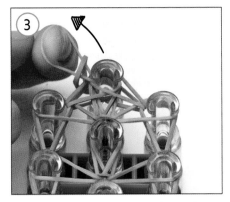

Grab the front loop—the one that is closest to the hook end of the hook—and pull it off the hook, keeping it on your finger. Slide the remaining loop off the hook, and then pull the loop on your finger to tighten the knot.

ADDING LINKS FOR LENGTH

Some projects, because of band arrangement or beads, don't have as much stretch as others. If a piece like a bracelet comes up short, you can simply add basic links to extend the bracelet. Adding basic links is an easy solution. (If you can plan ahead and have two looms, your other option is to make the bracelet longer by combining two looms; see below.) Follow these steps to extend the length of a piece.

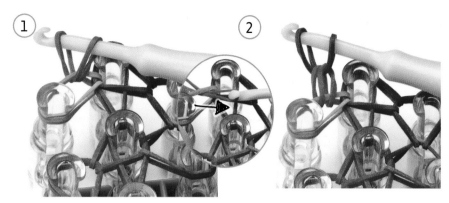

① Pull one end of a new band through the final band or set of bands where you want to extend the bracelet, just as you would when making a basic link (see page 19). Loop the end of the band you are holding up onto the hook.

② Keep adding links this way as needed.

COMBINING LOOMS

You can combine many looms end-to-end (lengthwise) or side-to-side (widthwise) to make longer or wider projects. Most looms are easy to combine lengthwise (far right), but not all looms can be correctly combined widthwise. To make the Triple Cuff in this book, for example, you will need to combine your looms with the pegs in an alternating pattern (left); a Rainbow Loom® can be arranged this way. Note: You can't just place two looms next to one another and not change the peg columns around (middle)—that won't work.

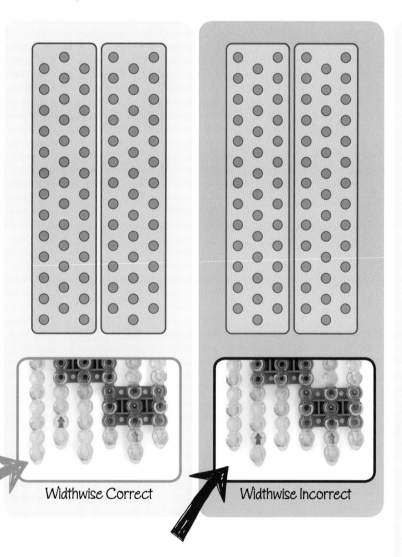

Widthwise Correct

Widthwise Incorrect

Lengthwise Correct

Making the Basic Bracelet on a Loom

This basic bracelet introduces you to the loom and the general idea of placing bands and looping them. It's the best way to learn how to use the loom before proceeding to the more challenging projects. Check out the helpful diagram on page 13 as you follow these step-by-step instructions.

MATERIALS: 25 RUBBER BANDS • 1 CLIP

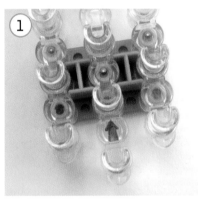

1

Turn your loom so that the arrow faces **up** (away from you); the bottom middle peg sticks out at the bottom.

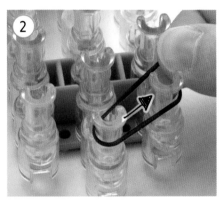

2

Place your first rubber band on the bottom middle peg (the one closest to you) and stretch it onto the bottom right peg.

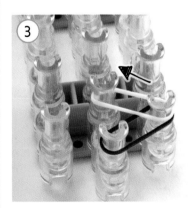

3

Place your second rubber band on the peg you just ended on and stretch it onto the peg to the upper left (the middle peg second from the bottom).

4

Place your third rubber band on the peg you just ended on and stretch it onto the peg to the upper right of it.

5

Keep on repeating this back-and-forth pattern until you've run out of bands or reached the top of the loom. **Always remember to start on the last peg you ended on.** Now look at the diagram and photo on page 13 and make sure that your loom looks like the pictures.

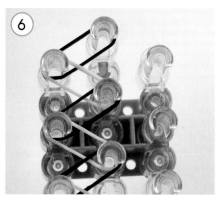

Now you are ready to loop. First, turn your loom so that the arrow at the top is facing **down** (toward you).

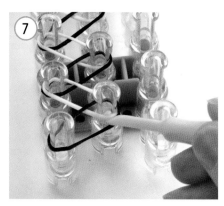

Starting at the bottom of the loom (closest to you), **push your hook down into the big loop** created by the last band you placed. Hook the second-to-last band you placed, being sure to hook it **inside the groove** on the peg.

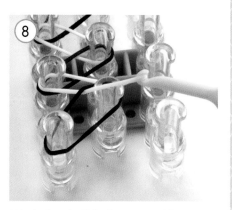

Lift the band off the bottom middle peg…

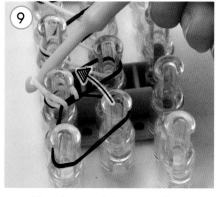

…and loop it around the peg to the upper left, which is the other peg that the band is also looped on. This is looping a band back to the peg it came from.

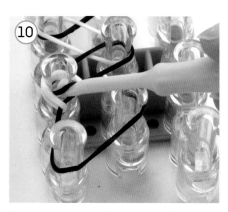

Now, push your hook down into the groove in the peg you just looped onto, and hook the next rubber band. Don't hook the one you just looped!

Never hook a band by going around the outside as shown in this photo. **ALWAYS** push your hook down into the groove of the peg you are on, down inside the bands that are already looped there, as shown in step 10.

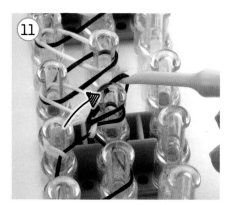

Lift the band off the peg and loop it back to the peg it came from.

12

Keep on repeating this pattern all the way up to the top of the loom. **Always remember to push your hook down into the groove before hooking the next band.** Here's what your loom should look like after you finish all the looping. Stick with it; soon it'll become like second nature.

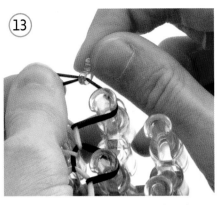

13

Take your clip and hook it around **both strands** of the one rubber band that is looped on the top middle peg, the very last band that you looped. It helps to pull the strands taut with one finger.

14

Holding the clip firmly between your fingers, pull the bracelet off the loom, one peg at a time. Don't be afraid to pull hard; it won't break.

15

Clip the rubber band on the other end onto the clip. This is when you can replace the clip with a jewelry finding to really pull the piece together.

CRAFTY TIP: COLORS GALORE

You can get creative with color on the very first bracelet you make. The order of your bracelet colors will match the order you place the rubber bands on the loom. If you alternate colors, you'll have an alternating bracelet; if you do three of one color at a time, you'll have stripes along your bracelet. Try laying out your 25 rubber bands in the pattern you want to see.

Understanding Diagrams

Now that you've made a basic bracelet, let's look at the diagram for the basic bracelet so that you will be able to use the diagrams in this book. For most projects, there is a **Load It Up** diagram that you must follow in order to get your bracelet or other project started. This is called loading it or placing it on the loom. Then, you simply follow the step-by-step Get Looping instructions to make your bracelet. It's that easy.

The **Load It Up** diagram shows you the order in which you must place your rubber bands and how your loom will look once you have finished placing all your bands. Each diagram shows a specific color arrangement; you can always change the colors, but never change the order.

LOAD IT UP

Take a look at this **Load It Up** diagram for the basic bracelet. If you followed the step-by-step directions on page 10, then you followed this pattern the whole way through. Your loom should look just like the photo of the loaded loom to the right. Try making another basic bracelet by following the diagram and see if you succeed.

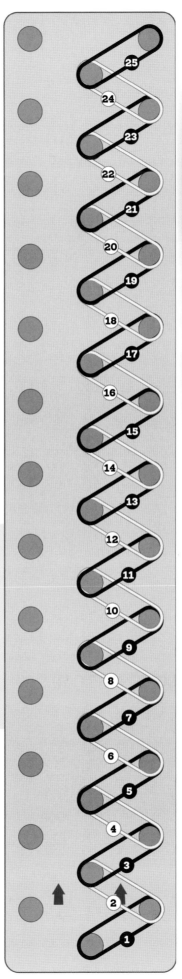

Start at this end

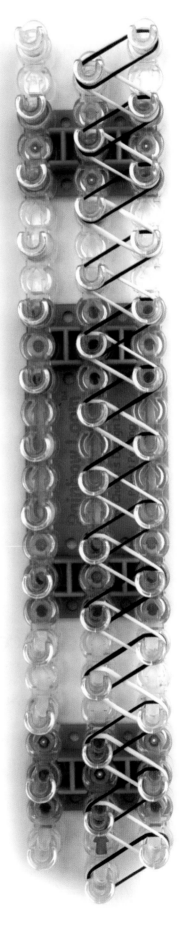

Basic Link Love

>>BASIC

The bracelet that started it all takes less than three minutes to make once you master the technique of making basic links on the hook, which is faster than making basic links on the loom. With an average of just 25 bands, you can buy one pack of bands and then make tons of basic link bracelets for you and your friends. Plus, the basic bracelet is great for stacking and for mixing in with other, bigger bracelets as a nice accent.

Technique on page

19

<<DOUBLE LINKS BRACELET

Achieve a totally different look with the same technique by making a basic link bracelet with two links at once instead of one, using 50 bands. This makes the bracelet thicker and more solid and gives you more room to play with mixing colors.

>>METAL LINKS BRACELET

This sophisticated look is easy as pie. Just alternate rubber band links with metal jump rings or other jewelry findings that can be opened and closed. Be careful, though: the higher the ratio of metal links to rubber band links, the less stretchy the bracelet will be, and forcing it to stretch may pull weak jump rings apart, ruining your bracelet. If you want to make a bracelet with a three-to-one jump ring to rubber band ratio, for example, you'll want to use a real jewelry closure to connect the ends, because the bracelet won't safely stretch over your hand.

<<DANGLY CHAIN EARRINGS

Create simple but sweet earrings by hanging basic chains from a French hook earring. You can make one long chain, three long chains, three chains of mixed length, chains with beads on the end, chains with multiple beads... the possibilities are endless. Just make sure when you loop the bands onto the earring hook that you close the hook tightly with jewelry pliers, because the bands try to slide off if you don't. The first band in a beadless dangly chain earring should be a wrapped bead band; see the steps for filler bead bands on page 33.

<<LINKED HOOP EARRINGS

Use two bands at once to make a straight chain of bands (just like you do when making a double links bracelet). Then shape the chain into a circle and loop both ends onto a French hook earring. Make two more hoops this way, linking them together around each other and knotting them closed with some super stretchy plastic thread or sewing thread of a matching color. You could also use findings like jump rings or clasps if you want to make the connections a visible part of the design. The earrings pictured used about 20 bands per hoop.

>>DROP PENDANT NECKLACE

To make a necklace with a drop pendant, start by threading your first band through the pendant. From that band, make the whole drop chain (working your way up toward the necklace), and then add a clip to the top band of the drop chain to mark your place. Make half of the necklace from that point, clip the end, and then return to the clipped band of the drop chain to make the other half of the necklace. All the connections are seamless! You might be tempted to make the necklace and then create the drop chain from the middle of it, but this won't work—you'll have to tie or use a jump ring to attach the pendant to the bottom band of the drop chain. The necklace pictured used 70 bands.

>>BEADED NECKLACE

Adding beads to a basic chain is a great way to doll it up. You can use this technique for simple bracelets, too. Start making your necklace on the hook. When you are ready to add a bead, thread a piece of thread through the loops that are currently on the hook, then remove the loops from the hook, leaving them secure on the thread. Next, use the thread to pull both loops of the band on the thread through a bead. It'll have to stretch quite a bit, but that's okay. Re-hook the two loops, and continue your basic chain. The necklace pictured used 60 bands and 20 beads.

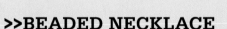

>>CHAIN NECKLACE

Shiny, hard chain is a great contrast to vivid, soft rubber bands. The two may be totally different, but they really complement one another. Take any wide-link metal chain you like the look of, and then thread a basic rubber band chain through the links. You can add an immediate, eye-catching pop of color to any outfit with this quick look. The necklace pictured used about 90 bands with a metal chain about 30" (76cm) long.

>>BRAIDED NECKLACE

This necklace may look like it took hours to make, but your secret is that it took fifteen minutes! To make a braided necklace, make three long basic link chains separately, each with about 90 bands. Then connect them at one end, braid the strands, and connect the other end when you finish. You can braid tightly or loosely for two different looks!

Basic Link Love

MATERIALS: 25 BANDS • 1 CLIP

GET LOOPING

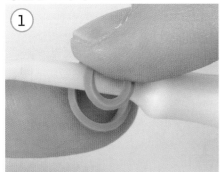

① To start a basic link, first fold one band over your hook as shown.

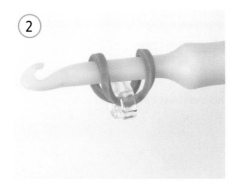

② Clip the two loops to secure the band around your hook.

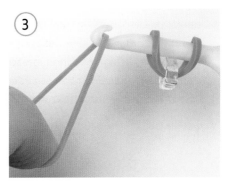

③ Hook one end of your second band on the tip of the hook, holding the other end with one finger so it is slightly taut.

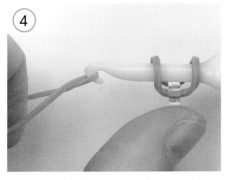

④ Rotate your hook so it faces down, making sure the clipped band doesn't rotate. Your hook and bands should look like this. Twisting your hook lets it slide through the clipped band without getting caught on the two loops.

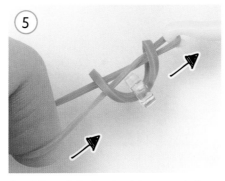

⑤ Carefully pull the hook, with one end of the second rubber band, all the way back through the double loop, holding onto the other end of the second band with your fingers. Don't pull the end you're holding through the double loop.

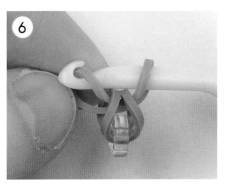

⑥ Rotate the hook so it faces up. Then loop the end of the band you are still holding up onto the hook. Make sure the band isn't twisted. The first clipped band will end up underneath the hook.

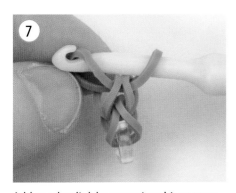

⑦ Add another link by repeating this process (steps 3–6) of hooking a new band, twisting your hook down, pulling the band through, twisting your hook up, and looping the other end of the band onto the hook.

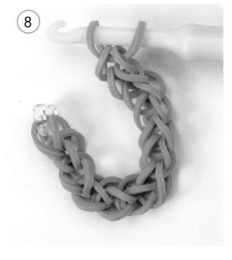

⑧ Now continue making as many links as you need to! You can even make an entire bracelet this way by making 25 basic links in a row.

Fishtail

>>BASIC

The basic fishtail design is a staple. It has a nice, solid heft, can be made quickly, combines well with other bracelets, and stacks great. The look of the fishtail also makes it one of the most popular designs for men. Every maker of rubber band jewelry must know how to make the basic fishtail—and why wouldn't you want to?

Technique
on page
25

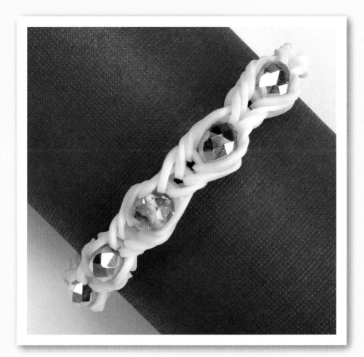

<<BEADED BRACELET

As you are making your fishtail, add beaded bands in a regular pattern. Know that adding beads to a fishtail design makes the bracelet longer, so you'll need fewer bands to create a comfortable bracelet—about 30–40 instead of 50, depending on how big the beads are and how many you use.

>>STACKED CUFF

A great way to achieve different effects with the fishtail design is to stack them together. You can mix and match colors and patterns to create infinite variations only limited by the number of single fishtail bracelets you've made. So get cracking!

>>HALF CHAIN

This cool, modern design is half fishtail and half metal chain. Depending on the quality and size of the chain you use, you may need some heavy-duty jewelry pliers, but the effect is totally worth the extra effort. Just connect each end of the fishtail piece to each end of a short length of chain. For the half-and-half effect, make your fishtail piece about 21 bands long and your metal chain about 4" (10cm) long.

<<CHARM BAND

The fishtail is a handy design if you have a pendant or charm that you'd like to turn into a bracelet. Loop the first band of the fishtail through the charm before placing it onto the pegs and continuing the design. Just make half of the bracelet this way, so that when you place the charm on the top of your wrist, the bracelet comes halfway around your wrist. Take the piece off the loom and clip. Now repeat for the other side: loop the first band of the fishtail through the charm before placing it onto the pegs, and make the second half of the bracelet. When you're done, connect the two ends. Depending on the size of the charm, each fishtail half may be about 15 or more bands.

Try adding a black ribbon to the closure of the necklace for a beautiful, elegant finishing touch.

<<MOD HOOP NECKLACE

This necklace uses metal wire threaded through the bands to create a more solid shape. The metal will almost disappear in the middle of the bands, but gleam through when it catches the light. To incorporate the wire core, first place the first three bands of the necklace on the loom. Then, cut a piece of wire about 6" (15cm) longer than the size you want your finished necklace to be (this necklace is 16" [40cm] finished), and thread it up through the center of the three bands. Then bend the top of the wire into a wide hook—this will prevent it from falling out through the bottom of the piece. Every time you add a band to the loom, make sure to loop it all the way around the wire hook so that the wire is always coming up through the center of it. Use real jewelry closures to connect the wire at each end of the necklace once it's completed. This necklace used about 250 bands.

Create a hook with the wire while looping to prevent it from sliding out.

Attach a jewelry clasp to the wire at each end.

⋏ BEADED EARRINGS

When starting a beaded fishtail earring, simply make the first band you place on the loom a beaded band. Then add bands and loop as you normally would. Try making an earring anywhere from 4 to 12 bands long.

<<SPIRAL STATEMENT NECKLACE

Making this stunning statement necklace requires more tools than many other pieces, but the effort is worth it! Make three fishtail chains of two different sizes (the ones pictured were made of 115 bands and 45 bands). Then form the chains into spirals that are cozy but not too tight. Use ultra-thin, stretchy plastic string to subtly tie the ends at the outsides of the spirals (it's practically invisible!). Then, cut a piece of felt backing and glue all three spirals to it. The rubber band material is tricky to glue, but a specialized glue for foam should do it. Complete the project with a matching basic link chain.

Fishtail

MATERIALS: 48 BANDS • 2 EXTRA BANDS • 1 CLIP

GET LOOPING

1 First place one rubber band in a figure eight shape around two pegs that are next to each other. Make sure the peg grooves face to the right, so the arrow on the loom faces to the right.

2 Place two more bands, one at a time, on the same two pegs, without twisting them into figure eights.

3 Hook the bottom band to the left of where it crosses for the figure eight.

4 Loop it up and off the peg it's looped on, letting it go in the center.

5 Do the same with the bottom band to the right side, looping it off the peg and letting it go in the center.

6 Now the bottom band is securely looped around the other two bands.

7 Push the two bands on the pegs down toward the bottom of the loom without pushing them against each other. Then add another band to the two pegs, without twisting it.

8 Unloop the new bottom band as you did the first band, one side at a time.

9 Push the bands down, add another band, and unloop the new bottom band. Repeat until you reach the desired length. As you go, tug on the base of the bracelet.

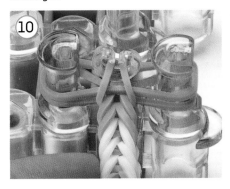

10 The last two bands aren't part of your final piece, so don't factor them into your pattern. Clip the last band you unlooped, making sure to hook both strands of the band.

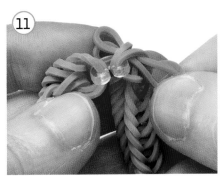

11 Slide the bracelet off the pegs and pull the two final loose bands out. Use jewelry clasps or other findings to connect the ends.

Vine

>>BASIC

The vine design can look unique and funky when the rings are made of single bands, or it can look classy and almost Celtic when the rings are made of three bands or single twisted bands. And beads can take the vine to a more fun level, too. This bracelet fits the average wrist well with just one loom load, so whip it up quickly when you need a perfect accent for any outfit at the last minute.

Technique
on page
28

>>TWISTED RINGS

To make twisted rings and a slim bracelet, just twist the ring bands into figure eights when placing them on the loom. The result is really cool.

<<MULTI-BAND RINGS

Three bands are better than one! Try making your vine bracelet with three bands for each ring. It will pull the bracelet a little wider than if you use just one band, giving it a subtle but noticeably different look than the basic vine. Try mixing the colors of the three bands. Two bands also work well.

>>BEADED BRACELET

You can achieve a youthful or mature effect by adding different beads to the ring bands of the vine design. The types of beads you choose will also subtly change the shape of the bracelet as a whole: large, chunky beads will make the bracelet wider, whereas several small beads per ring will lengthen and thin the bracelet.

Vine

MATERIALS: 34 BANDS (VINE) • 10 BANDS (RINGS) • 1 CLIP

LOAD IT UP

First, place the 34 "vine" bands as shown in the diagram. It's like a zigzag, but with an extra up-and-down band at each corner. Once you've placed all 34 vine bands, add the "ring" bands where shown to fill in the holes, starting with band 35 near the bottom of the loom.

GET LOOPING

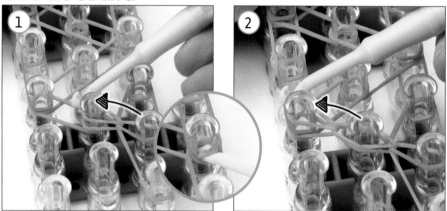

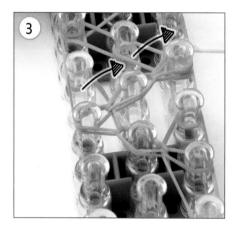

Turn the loom so the arrow faces down. Hook the bottom band on the second from bottom right peg and loop it up to the second from bottom middle peg. Be sure to push your hook down into the peg, inside the last ring band you placed, to hook the band.

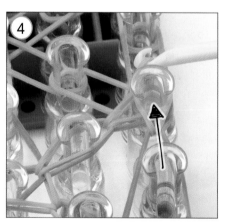

Push your hook down into the peg and hook the bottom band on the second from bottom middle peg, where you just ended. Loop it to the peg to the upper left of it.

Then, starting from the peg you just ended on, loop the next two bottom bands diagonally up and to the right, like you did in steps 1–2.

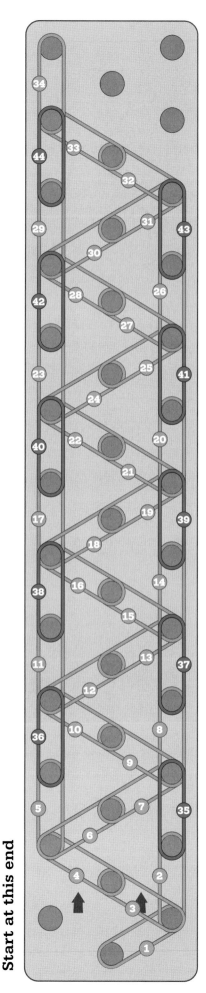

Now loop the band from the third from bottom right peg up to the fourth from bottom right peg. This is the band that shares a peg with the top of the ring band closest to you. The ring bands do not get looped.

This diagram shows the Rainbow Loom®, but if you are using a different loom, don't worry: follow the diagram and instructions exactly and your piece will turn out great. You may just have unused pegs.

Start at this end

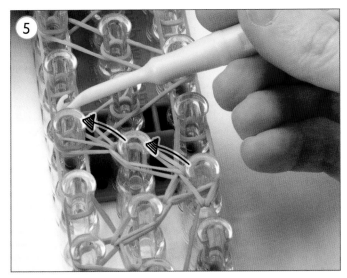

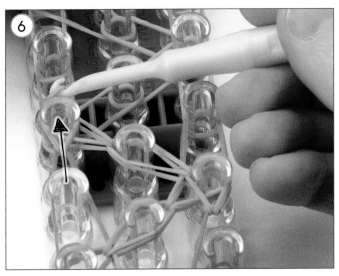

Now, starting from the peg you just ended on, loop the next two bottom bands, diagonally up and to the left, like you did in step 3. The first band goes from the right column to the center column; the second band goes from the center column to the left column.

As in step 4, loop the band that shares a peg with the top of the second ring band up to the peg above it. This is looping the band from the fourth from bottom left peg to the fifth from bottom left peg.

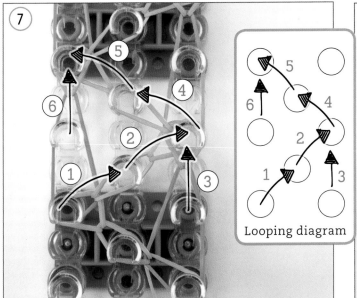

Looping diagram

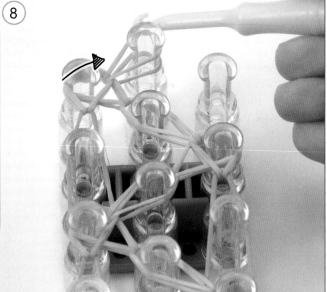

Repeat the pattern in steps 3–6 for the rest of the bracelet, following the zigzag path you made when you placed the bands. Always loop two bands diagonally up and across ①②, then loop up the band that connects the next ring band ③. Use the looping diagram as a guide.

Loop the bottom band from the top left peg to the top middle peg, push your hook down through the final bands, and pull your bracelet off the loom. Use jewelry clasps or other findings to connect the ends.

Ladder

>>BASIC

The ladder design can be quick to make if you use fewer, bigger beads, or it can take a little while if you use many smaller beads, but either way, the effect is spectacular. Try using many small beads at once, or one really long tube bead, or mix up a whole bunch of different beads. You're only limited by the number of beads you have on hand!

Technique on page
32

>>MIXED BAND BEADS

If you want to use fewer beads and have them really stand out, try making "band beads" out of three rubber bands each, and then mix them in with beaded bands. See the instructions for the technique on page 33 to make the band beads.

<<DOUBLE LADDER

You can make this stunning design by connecting two looms side by side and using five of the columns, with the outer and center peg columns for the band columns and the beaded bands strung between them. You can also achieve two looks with the same bracelet by putting it on and either aligning the two columns or adjusting the bracelet so that they create a chevron design (as styled on page 30).

<<STAGGERED DOUBLE LADDER

Make this airy design by connecting two looms side by side and using five of the columns, with the outer and center columns for the band columns. Unlike the double ladder design, though, stagger your beaded bands, leaving every other row empty.

Ladder

MATERIALS: 23 BEADED BANDS • 48 BANDS • 2 CLIPS

LOAD IT UP

Load bands up the entire left side, then the entire right side. Then add 11 beaded bands, like the rungs of a ladder, where shown, skipping the top and bottom rows.

GET LOOPING

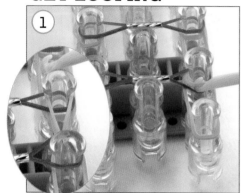

Turn the loom so the arrow faces down. Hook the bottom band on the second from bottom right peg, and loop it to the peg above it. Make sure you push your hook down into the peg to hook the band.

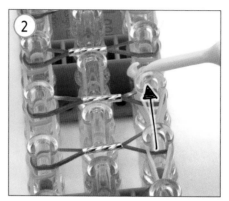

Hook the bottom band on the peg you just ended on and loop it to the peg above it. Loop the entire right side this way. Always make sure you push your hook down into the peg, inside the beaded band.

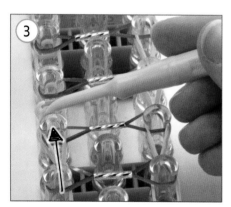

Now, starting at the second from bottom left peg, loop the entire left side as you did the right side.

Clip each of the bands at the top of the loom, and pull the piece off the loom.

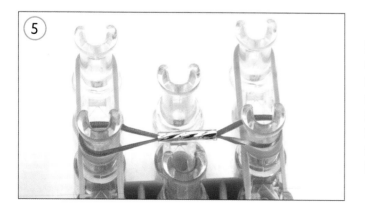

Reload the loom as you did the first time, using 11 of the 12 beaded bands you have left, skipping the top and bottom rows.

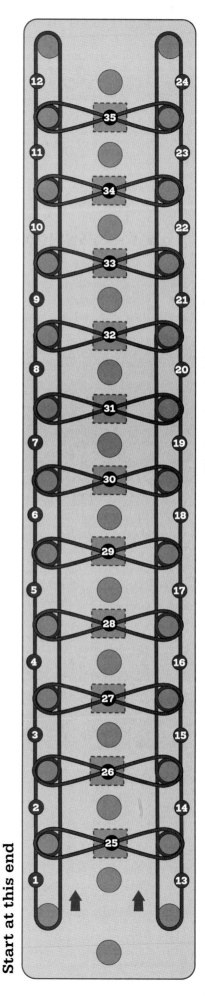

This diagram shows the Rainbow Loom®, but if you are using a different loom, don't worry: follow the diagram and instructions exactly and your piece will turn out great. You may just have unused pegs.

Start at this end

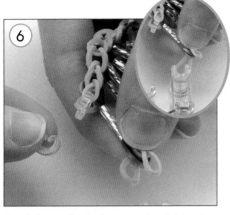

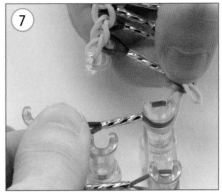

Carefully unclip the band on the right side of the piece you already made, pinching the band at its base securely between two fingers so that it doesn't slide through. Place the bottom loop of the band onto the top right peg of the loom. Don't let go of the band.

Still holding onto the band, place one side of the final beaded band onto the top right peg.

MAKING FILLER BAND BEADS

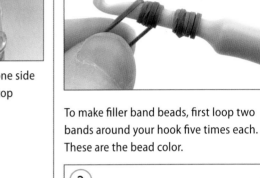

To make filler band beads, first loop two bands around your hook five times each. These are the bead color.

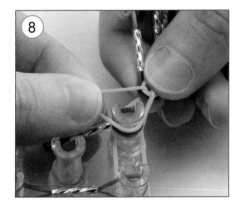

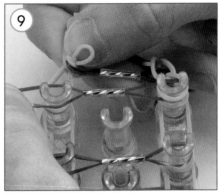

Place the top loop of the band you are holding onto the top right peg. Attaching the piece this way will make the transition between the two halves of the bracelet seamless.

Attach the left half of the piece to the top left peg the same way: unclip the band, place the bottom loop, place the second half of the beaded band, and place the top loop.

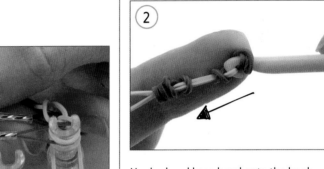

Hook a bead base band onto the hook and twist the hook upside down so that the base band twists into a figure eight. Holding the base band taut, use one or two fingers to start carefully rolling the loops of the bands on the hook off the tip of the hook and onto the base band.

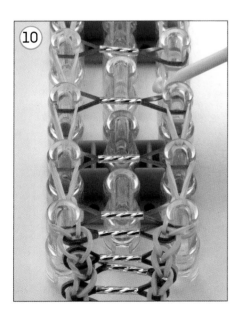

Turn your loom so the arrow faces down and loop the bracelet just as you did the first time, but this time starting from the very bottom pegs. Clip each of the top two bands and pull the bracelet off the loom. Use jewelry clasps or other findings to connect the ends, and cut off the two excess bands at the one end.

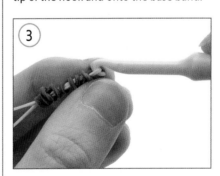

Do this for both bands on the hook. The last loop of each of the bands is the most difficult; you may need to use your thumb to pull it off the hook if it catches.

Nesting

>>BASIC

This design nestles beads within rubber bands for an interesting look. The basic nesting design can be elegant or funky depending on the types of beads you choose. Use small matching beads for a sophisticated look, or use a different vividly colored bead in every beaded segment for a more casual feel.

Technique on page

38

<<SIMPLE BEADLESS BRACELET

You can make the nesting design without any beads to achieve a subtle, knotted look. Here you can see one bracelet made with a single non-beaded band in the center of every segment, as well as a bracelet made with three non-beaded bands in the center of every segment. The colors peek through more or less depending on how many non-beaded bands you use. A good length for a bracelet like this is nine segments.

>>CHOKER

Make a chain of 16 beaded segments (not quite three full loom loads) and connect the ends. Check the fit around your neck and add any additional segments to get the fit just right. Make sure the necklace isn't too tight.

<<WRAPPED BRACELET

Make a long chain of 30 beaded segments (five full loom loads), and then wrap them around your wrist and connect the ends. For a more secure connection, create some basic links through all the rows of the bracelet where they align for the perfect fit. It takes a few minutes and you have to be careful not to drop stitches or let the rows loosen, but it's worth the effort.

>>EARRINGS

To make an earring, load one beaded segment onto your loom (including a beaded band) and loop it per the instructions on page 38. Add a link through the top bands as in step 6 of the instructions, and then remove the earring from the loom. Carefully place both loops of the top band onto a French hook earring; make sure you use jewelry pliers to close the hoop of the earring base snugly so the bands don't slide off.

^ STATEMENT RING

Load one beaded segment onto your loom, but before adding the beaded band, place two additional bands coming straight out of the top middle peg of the circle. Then place a double-wrapped band at the very top peg of those two additional bands. Now place the beaded band. Turn your loom so the arrow faces down; start by looping the bottom band from the bottom peg up (loop from inside the double-looped band), and work your way up toward the circle. Then loop the circle per the instructions on page 38. Add two links in a row through the top bands as in step 6 of the instructions, and remove the ring from the loom. Use a very small jewelry clasp or other finding to connect the ends.

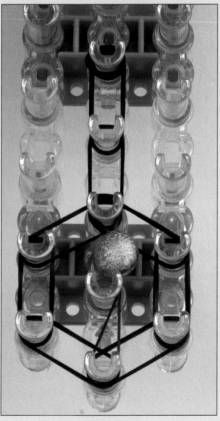

This is how you should load your loom for the ring. Don't forget the double-looped band at the very top.

Nesting

MATERIALS: 6 BEADED BANDS • 36 BANDS • 1 FINISHING BAND

LOAD IT UP

Place all the base bands as shown, doing one complete circle at a time. Then add all the beaded bands, connecting the two sides of the circles you formed.

GET LOOPING

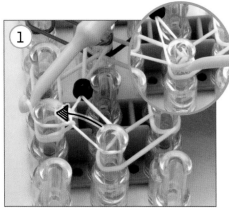

Turn the loom so the arrow faces down. Hook the second-from bottom band on the bottom middle peg and loop it up to the peg to the upper left of it. Be sure to push your hook down into the peg and hook the band from inside the wrapped bead band.

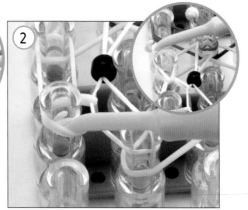

Hook the bottom band on the peg you just ended on and loop it up to the peg above it.

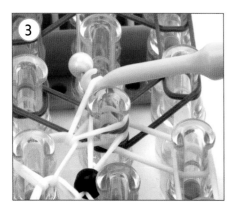

Hook the bottom band on the peg you just ended on and loop it to the peg to the upper right of it. This completes the left side of the circle.

Now loop the right half of the circle just as you looped the left half of the circle, starting with the bottom band on the bottom middle peg. Be sure to push your hook down into the peg and hook the band from inside the wrapped bead band.

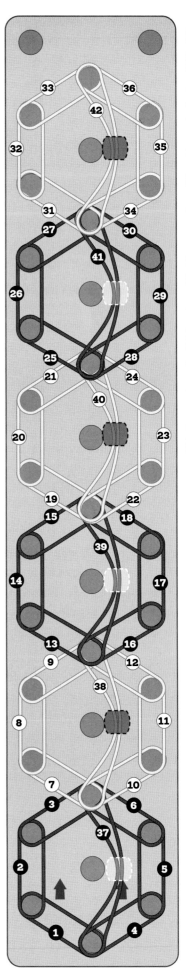

Start at this end

This diagram shows the Rainbow Loom® but if you are using a different loom, don't worry: follow the diagram and instructions exactly and your piece will turn out great. You may just have unused pegs.

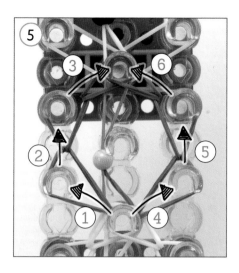

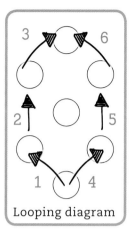

Looping diagram

Repeat the same looping pattern for the remaining five beaded segments of the bracelet. Be sure to always push your hook down into the peg to hook the bands. When hooking the first band of each circle from the bottom middle to the upper left, be sure to hook the correct band, the band that is second from bottom.

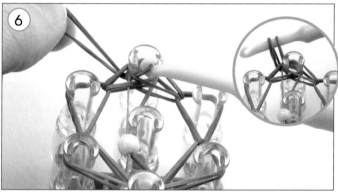

Once you have finished looping, push your hook down into the top middle peg, hook one new band, pull it up through, and create a normal link with the band through all the bands on the top middle peg.

Pull your bracelet off the loom and add any extra links you need for length. Use jewelry clasps or other findings to connect the ends.

LENGTHENING THE DESIGN

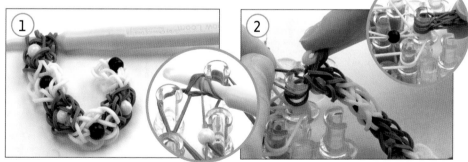

To make a longer bracelet or a necklace, make the basic bracelet following the directions through step 5. When you reach step 6, instead of creating a link through all the bands on the top middle peg, just push your hook down into the peg, secure all the bands on the hook, and pull the piece off the loom. Set the hook with the piece still attached aside, making sure none of the bands fall off.

Load the loom again as you did to make the first piece. If you have a color pattern, make sure it will line up correctly with the piece you already made. Then transfer all the bands from your hook down onto the top middle peg. Transfer one band at a time so that you don't drop any.

Now turn you loom so the arrow faces down and your first piece is attached at the bottom, closest to you. Loop all the bands just as you did the first time. Repeat this process as many times as you need to make your final piece the length you want.

Triple

>>BASIC

One of the most popular, talked-about rubber band bracelet designs is the triple. And it's popular for a reason! It has a nice, flat finish, is versatile for color mixing, and is straightforward to make. It's a sure bet when you want to make a bracelet for a friend, too.

Technique on page
43

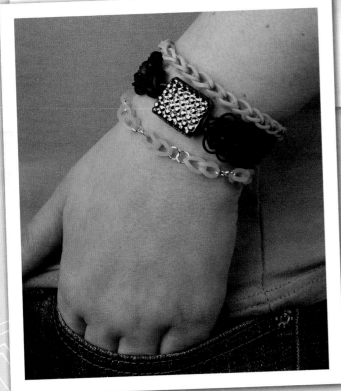

⌃ CHARM BAND

The triple makes a great watch band or band for a bracelet made with a charm. It will require some finagling and moving of bands, but simply load your loom once, turn the loom so the arrow faces you, and start looping your bottom row of three bands *through* the charm you want to attach. Depending on the size of your charm, you'll probably only need to load your loom with 9 or so rows instead of the full 12; 12 rows on each side will make the bracelet too big. Load so that your final loaded row is at the very top of the loom; this makes it easier to get the charm on. Looping the first row of bands through the charm might mean doing one band at a time and lifting the very first bands off the loom early so that you can move your charm where it needs to go and get all three bottom bands onto it, because most charms won't be wide and square like the end of the loom. Play with it, and you'll figure it out.

<<PENDANT NECKLACE

Follow the Alternate Finishing instructions on page 44 to make a long, continuous triple design. For a symmetrical necklace with the connection at the neck, far away from the pendant, start the bands at the pendant as described for the Charm Band project, and do four loom loads per half out from the pendant, for a total of eight loom loads. Then connect the ends.

>>BELT

Follow the Alternate Finishing instructions on page 44 to make a long, continuous triple design. A belt for your jeans will take about ten loom loads; a belt for your waist will take fewer. Slide a belt buckle or other accessory onto the belt before connecting the ends if you want to dress it up. Or you can just connect the ends; if you're wearing pants, the connection spot will be hidden underneath your belt loop anyway.

Start at this end

Triple

MATERIALS: 36 BANDS (MAIN COLORS) · 12 BANDS (BASE BANDS) · 1 FINISHING BAND

LOAD IT UP

Place rubber bands up each of the three columns, one column at a time. Then, place the base rubber bands around each set of three pegs as shown, forming triangles. Remember to skip the bottom set of three.

GET LOOPING

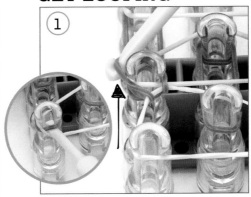

Turn the loom so the arrow faces down. First, hook the band from the bottom left peg and loop it onto the peg directly above it. Make sure you push your hook down into the groove and hook it from inside the base band as shown (inset).

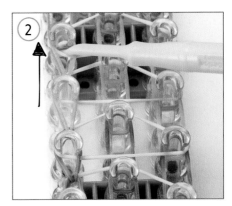

Loop the entire left column the same way as you did the first band, making sure to hook each band down in the groove from inside the base bands, not around the outside of the base bands.

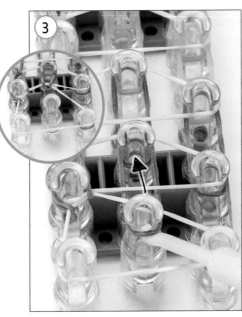

Next, starting at the bottom middle peg band, loop the entire middle column the same way.

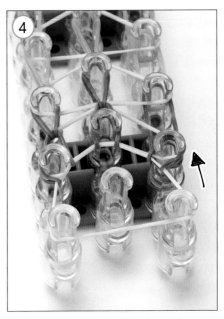

Then, loop the entire right column the same way. Make sure you hook each band down in the groove from inside the base bands, not around the outside of them.

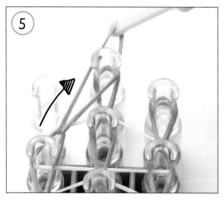

At the very top of the loom, hook the two strands off the top left peg and loop them onto the top middle peg.

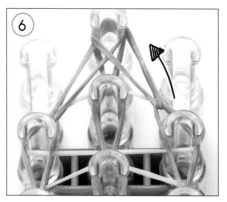

Do the same for the top right, hooking both strands from the top right peg and looping them onto the top middle peg. Now you have six strands of band on the top middle peg.

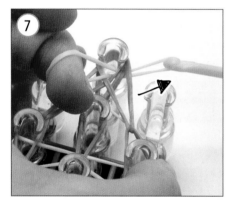

Now, make a slip knot (see page 8) with the finishing band around all the rubber bands on the top middle peg.

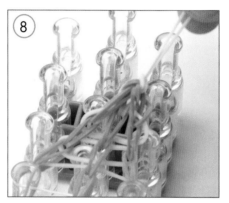

Pull your bracelet off the loom. Use jewelry clasps or other findings to connect the ends.

ALTERNATE FINISHING

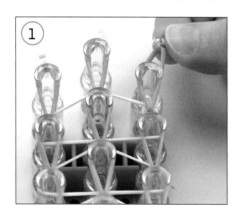

If you want a bracelet that circles your whole wrist without the thin stretched bands connecting the ends, follow steps 1–4 only, then add a clip to each of the three bands at the top of the loom. Remove the piece from the loom.

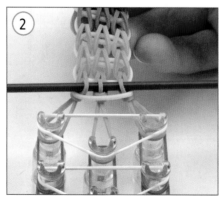

Reload your loom as you did the first time, then transfer the clipped bands from the first piece onto the loom following the instructions for the Triple Cuff on page 48.

Loop the bands on the loom as you did the first time, add a clip to each of the three bands at the top of the loom, and pull the bracelet off the loom. Connect the two ends with one set of clips.

Triple Cuff

>>BASIC

The basic triple cuff—made by doubling the design of the triple—has a great weight to it, and its width and simple shape make it a bold accessory that goes with anything. What else is that bold and versatile?

Technique on page 47

<<BEADED CUFF

To create a beaded cuff, first load your loom just as you would when making a regular cuff. Bead 22 bands, and then place them on the outer columns of the loom, folding both loops of each beaded band onto one peg with the bead facing out. For the first loom load, use 22 beaded bands: don't load beaded bands on the top or bottom rows of pegs. For the second loom load, use 24 beaded bands: don't load beaded bands on the bottom row of pegs, and incorporate beaded bands on the top row of pegs between steps 7 and 8 of the instructions.

Place beaded bands onto single pegs as shown.

>>COLOR IDEAS

There are a number of great ways to color your cuff. A chevron design is fashion-forward and easy to plan out. You can do long stripes, color blocks, a rainbow, or solids. The base bands are also a great way to change up subtle colors and tones in your cuff. Have fun with it!

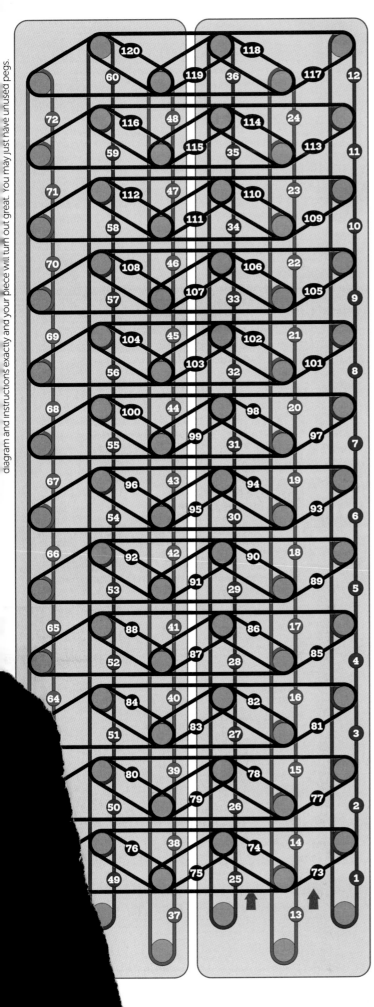

diagram and instructions exactly and your piece will turn out great. You may just have unused pegs.

Start at this end

Triple Cuff

MATERIALS: 144 BANDS (MAIN COLORS) · 96 BANDS (BASE BANDS) · 6 CLIPS

LOAD IT UP

Make sure your connected looms look exactly like the diagram, with the pegs all staggered. First load all of the bands up each of the six columns (bands 1–72). Then add the connecting triangle bands around three pegs, one at a time. Notice that you start on the bottom right side with a triangle whose point faces down (band 73); then place the next triangle with its point facing up (band 74); then the next triangle with its point facing down (band 75); then the last triangle in the row with its point facing up (band 76). See the illustration below to help you understand.

Bands 1–72

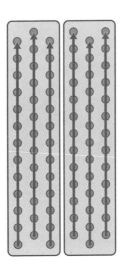

Bands 73–120

See below: Overlapping Triangles

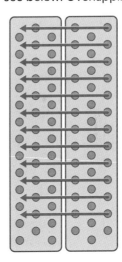

Overlapping Triangles

GET LOOPING

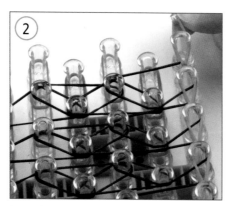

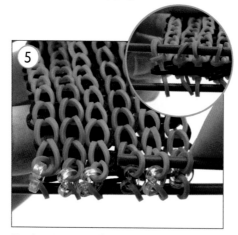

Turn the loom so the arrow faces down. Just like the Triple bracelet (page 43), hook the bottom band on the bottom right peg, making sure to push your hook down into the groove (inside the triangle band). Loop it to the peg directly above it.

Loop the entire right column this way, always making sure to push your hook down into the groove, inside the triangle bands. When you finish the column, clip the final band on the top peg.

Hook and loop all five remaining columns this way, clipping the final band at the top of each column. Always make sure to push your hook down into the groove, inside the triangle bands. When you are done looping, carefully pull the piece off the loom, going one peg at a time until you can get a good grip on all the bands at once.

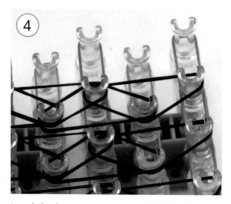

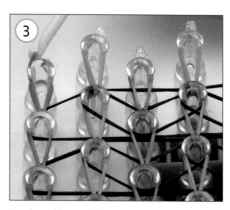

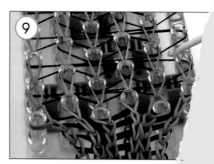

Load the loom again as you did the first time, but don't add the row of base bands at the top of the loom.

On the piece you already made, feed a short straw through each of the six bottom loops of the six clipped links, as shown. Feed a second straw through each of the six top loops of the six clipped links. Then remove the clips, being careful not to let any loops slide off the straw.

One by one, being careful not to drop any loops, place each loop from the bottom straw onto each of the top six pegs on the loom. Be careful not to twist the loops as you place them. Remove the straw.

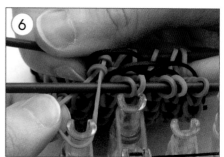

Now place the remaining four triangle base bands that you skipped on the top of the loom.

One by one, being careful not to drop any loops, place each loop from the top straw onto each of the top six pegs on the loom. Be careful not to twist the loops as you place them. Remove the straw.

Turn your loom so the arrow faces [...] loop all the bands as you did to m[...] first half of the cuff, clip the links [...] and remove the cuff from the l[...] jewelry clasps or other finding[...] the ends.